Lions, Lions!

The Story of Daniel

Any questions or comments about *God Loves Me?* We'd love to hear from you.

Faith Alive Christian Resources
1-800-333-8300
editors@faithaliveresources.org

We are grateful to early childhood educators Jesslyn DeBoer, Patricia Nederveld, Sherry Ten Clay, and Yvonne Van Ee for their contributions to *God Loves Me,* a Bible story program for young children. We are also grateful to Yu-Mei Han for illustrating this children's book.

Photo on page 5: iStockphoto; photo on page 20: Phil Degginger/Tony Stone Images.

ISBN 978-1-59255-851-3

10 9 8 7 6 5 4 3 2 1

Lions, Lions!

The Story of Daniel

PATRICIA L. NEDERVELD

ILLUSTRATIONS BY YU-MEI HAN

God Loves Me™

FAITH ALIVE® Christian Resources

Grand Rapids, Michigan

This is a story from
God's book, the Bible.

It's for say name(s) of your child(ren).
It's for me too!

Daniel 6

Hi! My name is Daniel. I have an important job! I work for my friend, the great King Darius.

But I pray to our great God. That's the most important thing I do. I pray to God three times every day.

There were some men who wanted to hurt me. They made a rule that people everywhere should pray only to King Darius—not to our great God.

Well, praying to people is wrong. Of course I couldn't do that. So I still prayed to our great God. When those men saw me pray, they grabbed me and threw me into a cage filled with lions!

I guess those men
thought the lions
would hurt me.
They didn't know
that our great God
could keep me safe.

Can you see how
God kept me safe?

My friend, King Darius, didn't know that God could keep me safe either. The next day he came to see what happened inside the lions' cage. "Daniel! Daniel! Did your God keep you safe?" he called.

“Yes, O King! My God can do great things. I’m safe!” I called back.

You can see how happy the king was when he saw me!

Then King Darius made a new rule for all his people: Pray to Daniel's God, for Daniel's God is very great!

I wonder if you know that God loves you and cares for you too . . .

Dear God, thank you for keeping Daniel safe. Please take good care of us too. Amen.

Suggestions for Using This Book

In a Group Setting

Opening and Story Time

Gather your little ones around you and spend a few minutes talking about lions. (If you have a lion puppet, a stuffed toy lion, or a book about lions, bring it for the children to look at and touch.) Invite them to tell you about lions they've seen at the zoo, in movies, or on TV. Assure everyone that real lions live far away—or in the zoo. They're wild animals that God has made for us to learn about and enjoy watching—from a distance. Not close up, like Daniel did.

Show the children the cover of this book and wonder what's happening in the picture. Then read Daniel's story to the children, beginning on page 4 and inserting their names. Make sure everyone can see the pictures and go slowly, giving the children time to point to things that capture their imaginations or to respond to the story. You'll want to encourage everyone to respond to the question on page 21 too. End your story with the prayer printed there.

Learning Through Play

Learning through play is the best way. The suggestions listed here are meant to help you provide props and experiences that will invite your twos and threes to play their way into the Scripture story and its simple truth. Try to provide plenty of time for the children to choose their own activities and to explore and play individually, which is the way of young children! Use group activities sparingly—little ones learn most comfortably (and happily) with a minimum of structure.

- At your art table provide materials for making lion masks. You'll need 9-inch paper plates, lion faces (*God Loves Me* pattern 12), glue sticks, and lots of small squares torn from brown and tan construction paper. Help the children glue the face cutouts onto the center of their paper plates, then add lots of torn paper squares around the faces to make the lions' manes. (A simpler way: give the children crayons in shades of brown and gold and show them how to color the "manes.")
- Use chairs or blocks to make a lions' den in a corner of your room. Invite the children to pretend to be lions (using their masks if they've made them) and other animals they've seen in the zoo. (Be sensitive to little ones who might be frightened by being so close to the scary noises.) Use the children's play as an opportunity to remind everyone that God is with us, protecting us and taking good care of us.
- If your children look forward to music time, use the song "Who Did Swallow Jonah" (*Sing with Me Preschool Songs*, track 13) again this week. Spend a few minutes looking at the book and recalling the story together before listening to the song. Listen to the Daniel verse too, as you look at this storybook and recall the wonderful ways in which God

rescued both Jonah and Daniel. (Ask the children if they'd rather be rescued from the stomach of a big fish or a den of lions.) End your music time by dancing to "Come, Praise the Lord" (*Sing with Me Preschool Songs*, track 9).

- If your children enjoy playing hide-and-seek, try this variation with them—call it "Lion Hunt." You'll need two groups—the lions and the hunters. (Let the children choose which they'd rather be.) Ask the "lions" to find good hiding places while you and the "hunters" count slowly to ten. When you reach ten, call out: "Let the lion hunt begin!" The hunters must look for the lions and bring them back to a "cage" you've made with blocks or chairs.
- Bring a box of animal crackers for snack time and have a "lion hunt" by sorting through the crackers and separating out all of the lions. As you eat them up, remember the wonderful way God kept Daniel from being eaten up by the lions.
- Check out books about wild animals (especially lions) from your local library and set them out for the children to enjoy. Take time to read one or two to your little book lovers.

Closing

Call the children back together a few minutes before the end of their playtime—using a bell or music or a special rhyme works well. Make a circle, join hands, and close with a short prayer thanking God for watching over us and taking care of us no matter where we go (or repeat the prayer on page 21).

At Home

Try making "Lion Sandwiches" with your child this week. Using a round cookie cutter (or a plastic cup) cut circles from pieces of soft bread. Spread them with peanut butter (or soy butter) and make lion faces by adding banana slice ears, shredded cheese manes, and raisin eyes, noses, and mouths. Recall the story of Daniel as you work, marveling at the way in which our great God protected Daniel. Enjoy eating up the lions you've made, giving God the praise for protecting and caring for us every day.

Old Testament Stories

1 **Blue and Green and Purple Too!** *The Story of God's Colorful World*

2 **It's a Noisy Place!** *The Story of the First Creatures*

3 **Adam and Eve** *The Story of the First Man and Woman*

4 **Take Good Care of My World!** *The Story of Adam and Eve in the Garden*

5 **A Very Sad Day** *The Story of Adam and Eve's Disobedience*

6 **A Rainy, Rainy Day** *The Story of Noah*

7 **Count the Stars!** *The Story of God's Promise to Abraham and Sarah*

8 **A Girl Named Rebekah** *The Story of God's Answer to Abraham*

9 **Two Coats for Joseph** *The Story of Young Joseph*

10 **Plenty to Eat** *The Story of Joseph and His Brothers*

11 **Safe in a Basket** *The Story of Baby Moses*

12 **I'll Do It!** *The Story of Moses and the Burning Bush*

13 **Safe at Last!** *The Story of Moses and the Red Sea*

14 **What Is It?** *The Story of Manna in the Desert*

15 **A Tall Wall** *The Story of Jericho*

16 **A Baby for Hannah** *The Story of an Answered Prayer*

17 **Samuel, Samuel!** *The Story of God's Call to Samuel*

18 **Lions and Bears!** *The Story of David the Shepherd Boy*

19 **David and the Giant** *The Story of David and Goliath*

20 **A Little Jar of Oil** *The Story of Elisha and the Widow*

21 **One, Two, Three, Four, Five, Six, Seven!** *The Story of Elisha and Naaman*

22 **A Big Fish Story** *The Story of Jonah*

23 **Lions, Lions!** *The Story of Daniel*

New Testament Stories

24 **Jesus Is Born!** *The Story of Christmas*

25 **Good News!** *The Story of the Shepherds*

26 **An Amazing Star!** *The Story of the Wise Men*

27 **Waiting, Waiting, Waiting!** *The Story of Simeon and Anna*

28 **Who Is This Child?** *The Story of Jesus in the Temple*

29 **Follow Me!** *The Story of Jesus and His Twelve Helpers*

30 **The Greatest Gift** *The Story of Jesus and the Woman at the Well*

31 **A Father's Wish** *The Story of Jesus and a Little Boy*

32 **Just Believe!** *The Story of Jesus and a Little Girl*

33 **Get Up and Walk!** *The Story of Jesus and a Man Who Couldn't Walk*

34 **A Little Lunch** *The Story of Jesus and a Hungry Crowd*

35 **A Scary Storm** *The Story of Jesus and a Stormy Sea*

36 **Thank You, Jesus!** *The Story of Jesus and One Thankful Man*

37 **A Wonderful Sight!** *The Story of Jesus and a Man Who Couldn't See*

38 **A Better Thing to Do** *The Story of Jesus and Mary and Martha*

39 **A Lost Lamb** *The Story of the Good Shepherd*

40 **Come to Me!** *The Story of Jesus and the Children*

41 **Have a Great Day!** *The Story of Jesus and Zacchaeus*

42 **I Love You, Jesus!** *The Story of Mary's Gift to Jesus*

43 **Hosanna!** *The Story of Palm Sunday*

44 **The Best Day Ever!** *The Story of Easter*

45 **Goodbye—for Now** *The Story of Jesus' Return to Heaven*

46 **A Prayer for Peter** *The Story of Peter in Prison*

47 **Sad Day, Happy Day!** *The Story of Peter and Dorcas*

48 **A New Friend** *The Story of Paul's Conversion*

49 **Over the Wall** *The Story of Paul's Escape in a Basket*

50 **A Song in the Night** *The Story of Paul and Silas in Prison*

51 **A Ride in the Night** *The Story of Paul's Escape on Horseback*

52 **The Shipwreck** *The Story of Paul's Rescue at Sea*

Holiday Stories

Selected stories from the New Testament to help you celebrate the Christian year

24 **Jesus Is Born!** *The Story of Christmas*

25 **Good News!** *The Story of the Shepherds*

26 **An Amazing Star!** *The Story of the Wise Men*

43 **Hosanna!** *The Story of Palm Sunday*

44 **The Best Day Ever!** *The Story of Easter*

45 **Goodbye—for Now** *The Story of Jesus' Return to Heaven*

These fifty-two books are the heart of *God Loves Me,* a Bible story program designed for young children. Individual books (or the entire set) and the accompanying program guide can be ordered from Faith Alive Christian Resources at *www.faithaliveresources.org* or by calling 1-800-333-8300.